A Guide for Using

Charlie and the Chocolate Factory

in the Classroom

Based on the novel written by Roald Dahl

*This guide written by **Concetta Doti Ryan**
and illustrated by **Sue Fullam** and **Blanca Apodaca***

Teacher Created Resources, Inc.
6421 Industry Way
Westminster, CA 92683
www.teachercreated.com

ISBN: 978-1-55734-420-5

©*1993 Teacher Created Resources, Inc.*
Reprinted, 2008
Made in U.S.A.

Table of Contents

Introduction

A good book can touch our lives like a good friend. Within its pages are words and characters that can inspire us to achieve our highest ideals. We can turn to it for companionship, recreation, comfort, and guidance. It also gives us a cherished story to hold in our hearts forever.

In *Literature Units*, great care has been taken to select books that are sure to become good friends!

Teachers who use this literature unit will find the following features to supplement their own valuable ideas.

- A Sample Lesson Plan

- Pre-reading Activities

- A Biographical Sketch and Picture of the Author

- A Book Summary

- Vocabulary Lists and Suggested Vocabulary Activities

- Chapters grouped for study, with each section including:

    - *quizzes*

    - *hands-on projects*

    - *cooperative learning activities*

    - *cross-curriculum connections*

    - *extensions into the reader's own life*

- Post-reading Activities

- Book Report Ideas

- Research Ideas

- A Culminating Activity

- Three Different Options for Unit Tests

- Bibliography

- Answer Key

We are confident this unit will be a valuable addition to your planning and hope that as you use our ideas, your students will increase the circle of "friends" they can have in books!

Sample Lesson Plan

Each of the lessons suggested below can take from one to several days to complete.

LESSON 1

- Introduce and complete some or all of the pre-reading activities found on page 5.
- Read "About the Author" with your students. (page 6)
- Introduce vocabulary for Section 1. (page 8) Have students suggest definitions.

LESSON 2

- Read chapters 1–4. Place vocabulary in context and discuss meanings.
- Play a vocabulary game. (page 9)
- Write to a chocolate company. (page 11)
- Begin writing a fantasy story. (page 12)
- Discuss the book in terms of social studies. (page 13)
- Begin "Reading Response Journals." (page 14)
- Administer the Section 1 quiz. (page 10)
- Introduce vocabulary for Section 2. (page 8) Have students suggest definitions.

LESSON 3

- Read chapters 5–10. Place vocabulary in context and discuss meanings.
- Play a vocabulary game. (page 9)
- Design a golden ticket. (page 16)
- Conduct an interview. (page 17)
- Discuss the book in terms of social studies. (page 18)
- Make a family tree. (page 19)
- Administer the Section 2 quiz. (page 15)
- Introduce vocabulary for Section 3. (page 8) Have students suggest definitions.

LESSON 4

- Read chapters 11–17. Place vocabulary in context and discuss meanings.
- Play a vocabulary game. (page 9)
- Do personality profiles. (page 21)
- Continue writing fantasy story. (page 22)
- Discuss the book in terms of art. (page 23)
- Discuss moral issues. (page 24)
- Administer the Section 3 quiz. (page 20)
- Introduce vocabulary for Section 4. (page 8) Have students suggest definitions.

LESSON 5

- Read chapters 18–23. Place vocabulary in context and discuss meanings.
- Play a vocabulary game. (page 9)
- Make a prediction. (page 26)
- Complete fantasy story. (page 27)
- Discuss the book in terms of health. (page 28)
- Make chocolate recipes. (page 29)
- Administer the Section 4 quiz. (page 25)
- Introduce vocabulary for Section 5. (page 8) Have students suggest definitions.

LESSON 6

- Read chapters 24–30. Place vocabulary in context and discuss meanings.
- Play a vocabulary game. (page 9)
- Complete crossword puzzle. (page 31)
- Conduct a taste test. (page 32)
- Discuss the book in terms of language arts. (page 33)
- Make a class cookbook. (page 34)
- Administer the Section 5 quiz. (page 30)

LESSON 7

- Discuss any questions your students may have about the story. (page 35)
- Assign book reports and research projects. (pages 36 and 37)
- Begin work on culminating activities. (pages 38, 39, 40, 41, and 42)

LESSON 8

- Administer Unit Tests: 1, 2, and/or 3. (pages 43, 44, and 45)
- Discuss test possibilities and answers.
- Discuss student enjoyment of the book.
- Provide a list of related reading. (page 46)

Before the Book

Before you begin reading *Charlie and the Chocolate Factory* with your students, do some pre-reading activities to stimulate interest and enhance comprehension. Here are some activities that might work well in your class.

1. Predict what the story might be about just by hearing the title.

2. Predict what the story might be about just by looking at the cover illustration.

3. Discuss other books by Roald Dahl that students may have read or heard about.

   For example:

   Charlie and the Great Glass Elevator

   James and the Giant Peach

   Matilda

   The Witches

   Danny the Champion of the World

   Fantastic Mr. Fox

   See bibliography for more selections.

4. Answer these questions

   Are you interested in:

   – fantasy stories?

   – stories about chocolate?

   – stories in which the well-behaved child is rewarded?

   – stories about poor families who are saved?

   – stories about a boy and his grandpa?

   Would you ever:

   – enter a contest?

   – spend money you found in the street?

   – do something you were told not to do?

   – accept a very generous gift?

5. Work in groups or as a class to write a story about a poor family that wins a contest.

About the Author

Roald Dahl, pronounced Roo-aal Doll, was born September 13, 1916, and died in November 1990. He was born in Llandaff, South Wales, to Harold and Sofie Dahl. In 1953, he married actress Patricia Neal. They had five children, Olivia, Tessa, Theo, Ophelia, and Lucy. In 1983, they divorced and shortly thereafter Dahl married Felicity Ann Crosland.

Roald Dahl worked for Shell Oil Company in 1933–1939, spending the last two years in Tanzania. Dahl joined the Royal Air Force as a fighter pilot in 1939. In 1940, the plane he was flying was hit by enemy fire. Rescued by a fellow pilot, it took Dahl six months to recover from injuries to his head and nose. He rejoined his squadron in the spring of 1941 but soon was sent home on the disabled list. While in England, he was to be interviewed as someone who had seen action during the war. Through a turn of events he wound up writing the story himself. "A Piece of Cake" was published in *The Saturday Evening Post* and Dahl's career as a writer had begun.

As a writer Dahl had a prolific and varied career. He wrote and published short stories, poems, novels, movie and television scripts, and adaptations for both adults and children. *The Gremlins* was his first story for children. He wrote others, including *James and the Giant Peach* and *Danny the Champion of the World*. In 1964, *Charlie and the Chocolate Factory* was published. It has since become one of the most popular children's books in history. In 1971, it was adapted for the movies and was produced as *Willy Wonka and the Chocolate Factory*.

In writing for children, Dahl said, "Had I not had children of my own, I would have never written books for children, nor would I have been capable of doing so."*

More recently, Dahl had begun to produce autobiographical stories. In 1985, *Boy: Tales of Childhood* which contains memories of his childhood that he said he simply could not forget was published.

Dahl won numerous awards for his writing: Mystery Writers of America Award, the Edgar Award, the Whitebread Award, the World Fantasy Convention Lifetime Achievement Award, and the Federation of Children's Book Groups Award.

In talking about where he got his ideas for stories, Dahl said:

> *"I don't know where my ideas come from. Perhaps my Norwegian background is an influence. Plots just wander into my head. They are like dreams, one is terrified of losing them. Once I stopped the car and got out and wrote a word or two on the dust of the trunk lid so I wouldn't forget an idea.**

*Lee Bennett Hopkins, *More Books by More People*, Citation, 1974

**Contemporary Authors*, Volume 32

Charlie and the Chocolate Factory

by Roald Dahl

(Penguin, 1964; 1988)

(Available in Canada from Penguin, in U.K. and Australia from Penguin, Ltd.)

Charlie Bucket and his family are very poor. They barely have enough money to put food on the table. Things are even worse now that Mr. Bucket has lost his job at the toothpaste factory. The only happiness Charlie has is in the one single chocolate bar he receives every year on his birthday. This year's bar will be even more important because it could be the bar with the golden ticket.

Willy Wonka, the owner of the largest chocolate factory in the world, has decided to have a contest. He has hidden five golden tickets inside the chocolate bars. The five lucky people who find the tickets will be invited to be his guests at his factory for the day. In addition, they will receive enough candy to last them a lifetime.

Charlie is anxious to open his chocolate bar on his birthday. He desperately hopes to find a golden ticket inside. Charlie's entire family is distraught when there is no golden ticket inside. However, a few days later, luck is on Charlie's side. He finds a one dollar bill in the street. Although he feels guilty, he buys two chocolate bars. Inside the second one is a golden ticket.

Charlie and Grandpa Joe, along with four other children, visit the Wonka factory. Mr. Wonka is delighted to have them all there. However, he warns them that his factory is like a well-run machine and they should not touch anything without permission. Only Charlie Bucket heeds Willy Wonka's advice. The other four children get into terrible predicaments after doing things they were told not to do. Only Charlie Bucket is well behaved throughout the entire visit.

At the end of the day, Charlie and Grandpa Joe are the only ones still with Mr. Wonka. Then Willy Wonka confesses he is getting old and, therefore, designed the contest to find someone to take over the factory for him. He is so impressed with Charlie that he offers him the factory. Charlie is delighted. Mr. Wonka takes Charlie and Grandpa Joe in his great glass elevator to Charlie's house to get the rest of the family. They are all shocked when the elevator crashes through the roof of the house, and Mr. Wonka announces they are all moving to the factory where they will live happily ever after and never be hungry again.

Vocabulary Lists

On this page are vocabulary lists which correspond to each sectional grouping of chapters. Vocabulary activity ideas can be found on page 9 of this book.

SECTION 1
(Chapters 1–4)

draft	proper
desperately	greedily
inventor	furnace
belching	nightcap
absurd	eager
stammer	expose
faint	nibble
clever	colossal

SECTION 2
(Chapters 5–10)

dotty	glisten
enormously	frantically
youth	disappointed
ferociously	despicable
beckoned	ravenously
hooligan	revolting
repulsive	glint
vow	scraggy
criticize	stiletto

SECTION 3
(Chapters 11–17)

blissful	precious
sensation	verdict
dervish	procession
pandemonium	clustered
hallelujah	corridor
bulged	envious
peculiar	clatter
document	morsels
mystic	abide

SECTION 4
(Chapters 18–23)

glided	shriek
intense	furious
froth	
perched	journey
riverbank	yacht
astonish	balmy
scrambled	basin
rumbling	shalt
mist	mass

SECTION 5
(Chapters 24–30)

disturb	intently
wretched	frump
violently	staggered
scarlet	tantrum
despair	petrified
hollow	tremendous
rubbish	incinerator
cross	nudge
precipice	hovering

Vocabulary Activity Ideas

You can help your students learn and retain the vocabulary in *Charlie and the Chocolate Factory* by providing them with interesting vocabulary activities. Here are a few ideas to try.

❑ Challenge your students to a **Vocabulary Bee**! This is similar to a spelling bee, but in addition to spelling each word correctly, the game participants must correctly define the words as well.

❑ As a group activity, have students work together to create an **Illustrated Dictionary** of the vocabulary words.

❑ Play **20 Clues** with the entire class. In this game, one student selects a vocabulary word and gives clues about this word, one by one, until someone in the class can guess the word.

❑ Play **Vocabulary Charades**. In this game, vocabulary words are acted out.

❑ Encourage students to keep a **Vocabulary Journal** where they can list words they are unfamiliar with but did not appear on the vocabulary list.

❑ Have students locate the vocabulary words in the story. Then proceed to have them guess the meanings by using **Context Clues**.

❑ Challenge students to find **Synonyms or Antonyms** for the vocabulary words from within the story.

❑ Play **Vocabulary Concentration**. The goal of this game is to match vocabulary words with their definitions. Divide the class into groups of 2–5 students. Have the students make two sets of cards the same size and color. On one set have them write the vocabulary words. On the second set have them write the definitions. All cards are mixed together and placed face down on the table. A player picks two cards. If the pair matches the word with its definition, the player keeps the cards and takes another turn. If the cards don't match, they are returned to their places face down on the table, and another player takes a turn. Players must concentrate to remember the locations of the words and their definitions. The game continues until all matches have been made.

❑ Ask your students to make their own **Crossword Puzzles** or **Wordsearch Puzzles** using the vocabulary words from the story. Have them exchange papers and work the puzzle. When completed, the authors can correct the papers.

❑ Use the words and definitions to play **Bingo**. Fold an 8½" x 11" (22 cm x 28 cm) paper into 16 squares. Have students randomly write the words chosen for this activity in each space. The caller reads a definition and the players mark the correct word. Markers can be pieces of cut index cards, beans, or raisins. The first person to cover a row, column, or diagonal calls out "Bingo" and is the winner.

❑ Find the sentence in the book with the vocabulary word. Copy it. Rewrite the sentence by **Substituting a Synonym** which would make sense.

❑ Play **Hangman** using the definition as a clue. This might be a good activity to be played in partners.

Quiz Time!

1. On the back of this paper, write a one-paragraph summary of the major events in each of the chapters of this section.

2. Why can't Charlie's family afford to buy enough food or a larger, more comfortable house?

   _____

   _____

3. In spite of the difficult living situation, what tortures Charlie more than anything else?

   _____

   _____

4. Describe several of Willy Wonka's inventions. Which is your favorite? Why?

   _____

   _____

5. What happens to the house that Willy Wonka made for Prince Pondicherry?

   _____

   _____

6. What does Grandpa Joe think is odd about Willy Wonka's factory?

   _____

   _____

7. Why did Willy Wonka decide to close down his factory for a while?

   _____

   _____

8. Do you think that any of Willy Wonka's inventions could actually be created? Why or why not?

   _____

   _____

9. Describe the type of family Charlie has. Are they close? Do they get along?

   _____

   _____

10. Charlie's favorite food is chocolate. What is your favorite and why do you like it so much?

   _____

   _____

Consumer Correspondence

Many companies are willing to send information about their products if you simply write to them and ask. In fact, some companies have a specific department designated to handle consumer relations. Below are addresses for companies that produce products in which the chief ingredient is chocolate. Choose one of the companies and write a business letter to ask any questions you or your classmates may have about the product. Once you have mailed your letter you can expect to receive a response within six to eight weeks.

Follow the business letter format below or use the format given to you by your teacher.

---

your address
date
(skip line)

company address
(skip line)

Dear _____:
(skip line)

body of letter
(skip line between paragraphs)

(skip line before closing)

Sincerely,
(your signature)
your name

Addresses:

Hershey Chocolate	**Tootsie Roll Industries**	**Mars Inc./M & M**
Hershey, PA 17033-0815	Chicago, IL 60629	Hackettstown, NJ 07840
E.J. Brach Corporation	**Nestle Chocolate and Confection**	
4656 West Kinzie	Company Incorporated	
Chicago, IL 60644	Purchase, NY 10577	

NOTE: Address letters to *Attention: Consumer Relations*

Writing a Fantasy Story

(Part One: Setting)

Charlie and the Chocolate Factory is an excellent example of a fantasy story. As part of this unit of study, you and your classmates will be working in groups to write your own fantasy stories. This project will take place in three parts. In the first part, your group will determine the setting of the story. In studying Roald Dahl's use of descriptive language in writing about the chocolate factory you will learn to become more descriptive in your own writing. Be sure to save all your work from this section to use later in the unit.

Read the example below. In your group, discuss the reactions to Dahl's descriptions of the factory.

> *"It wasn't simply an ordinary enormous chocolate factory, either. It was the largest and most famous in the whole world! It was Wonka's factory, owned by a man called Mr. Willy Wonka, the greatest inventor and maker of chocolate that there has ever been. And what a tremendous, marvelous place it was! It had huge iron gates leading into it, and a high wall surrounding it, and smoke belching from its chimneys, and strange whizzing sounds coming from deep inside it. And outside the walls, for half a mile around in every direction, the air was scented with the heavy rich smell of melting chocolate!"*

Think about the setting of your fantasy story.

Where will your story take place? _____

_____

_____

When you picture the setting in your mind, what does it look like? _____

_____

_____

List some adjectives (describing words) you could use when describing the setting of the story.

_____   _____   _____

_____   _____   _____

_____   _____   _____

From Cocoa Bean to Chocolate

Those of us who love chocolate often think about how wonderful it would be if chocolate grew on trees. Well, surprisingly, it does! Chocolate is made from cocoa beans and cocoa beans grow on trees! Below are the steps used in making chocolate. Share them with your class. Then have students work alone or in groups to illustrate the steps. (The book *Cocoa Beans to Daisies* is an excellent resource for pictures of chocolate being processed.)

1. Cocoa trees grow where it is very hot, and they bear fruit three times a year. From these fruit pods, we get cocoa beans.

2. The fruit pods are taken off the trees when they are ripe. Inside each pod are about thirty to forty beans. After the beans are extracted from the pods, they are left out in the sun to dry. As they dry, they lose some of their bitter flavor.

3. Once the beans have dried, they are placed in large sacks. Since most of the countries that grow cocoa trees do not have chocolate factories, the beans are shipped to other countries for processing.

4. When the beans arrive at the factory they are very carefully cleaned. Then, they are roasted in large ovens. This roasting process brings out the flavor in the beans and makes the tough skin around the beans easier to remove.

5. The roasted beans are placed in a machine that takes off the hard skins. Then the machine grinds the beans. The crushed beans turn into a paste called cocoa butter. With a few additions, the cocoa butter is made into chocolate.

6. A machine adds milk, sugar, vanilla, and sometimes nuts and fruits to the cocoa butter. This mixture is placed in large vats where it is heated and stirred for several days until smooth.

7. Once the chocolate mixture is ready, it is poured into molds. The molds are shaken so the chocolate spreads evenly and to eliminate air bubbles. The molds pass through a cold tunnel which makes the chocolate hard.

8. Finally, the chocolate is packaged and sent to stores for purchase.

Reading Response Journals

One great way to ensure that the reading of *Charlie and the Chocolate Factory* touches every student in a personal way is to include the use of Reading Response Journals in your plans. In these journals, students can be encouraged to respond to the story in a number of ways. Here are a few ideas.

- Ask students to create a journal for *Charlie and the Chocolate Factory*. Initially just have them assemble lined and unlined three holed paper in a brad-fastened report cover with a blank page for the journal's cover. As they read the story, students may draw a design on the cover that helps tell the story for them.

- Tell students the purpose of the journal is to record their thoughts, ideas, observations, and questions as they read *Charlie and the Chocolate Factory*.

- Provide students with, or ask them to suggest, topics from the story that would stimulate writing. Here are a few examples from the chapters in Section 1.

   – Describe the challenges that Charlie faces in his everyday life.

   – Was there ever a time when you or your family faced a difficult struggle?

- After the reading of each chapter, students can write one or more new things they learned in the chapter.

- Ask students to draw their responses to certain events or characters in the story, using the blank pages in their journals.

- Tell students they may use their journals to record "diary-type" responses that they may want to enter.

- Encourage students to bring their journal ideas to life! Ideas generated from their journal writing can be used to create plays, debates, stories, songs, and art displays.

Allow students time to write in their journals daily. Explain to the students that their Reading Responses Journals can be evaluated in a number of ways. Here are a few ideas.

- Personal reflections will be read by the teacher, but no corrections or letter grades will be given. Credit is given for effort, and all the students who sincerely try will be awarded credit. If a "grade" is desired for this type of entry, you could grade according to the number of journals entries for the number of journal assignments. For example, if five journal assignments were made and the student conscientiously completes all five, then he or she should receive an "A."

- Nonjudgemental teacher responses should be made as you read the journals to let the students know you are reading and enjoying their journals.

Quiz Time!

1. On the back of the paper, write a one paragraph summary of the major events in each chapter in this section.

2. Why did Willy Wonka create the golden ticket contest?_____

_____

_____

3. Choose two of the children who found golden tickets and describe their personalities in detail.

_____

_____

4. Would you want to be friends with any of the children who found golden tickets? Why or why not?_____

_____

_____

5. Why does Grandpa Joe give Charlie a dime? _____

_____

_____

6. What does Charlie's family think of the children who found golden tickets? Why do you think they responded that way?_____

_____

_____

7. Why does Charlie have to walk slowly to school and stay inside during recess? _____

_____

_____

8. How does Charlie manage to get a dollar bill?_____

_____

_____

9. How is Charlie's life different or similar to your own? _____

_____

_____

10. Have you ever won a contest? Describe what the excitement of winning or the disappointment of losing feels like._____

_____

_____

Your Own Golden Ticket

The *Evening Bulletin* printed a copy of a statement made by Willy regarding his contest. In it, Willy Wonka explains that he has hidden five golden tickets inside his chocolate bars. The people who find the golden tickets will be invited to visit his factory and receive all the chocolate they can eat for the rest of their lives.

Imagine that Willy Wonka asked you to design the golden tickets he will use for his contest. What design would you use? Draw your version of the golden ticket below. Design both the front and back. You may write any information you feel is appropriate on the ticket. Be creative!

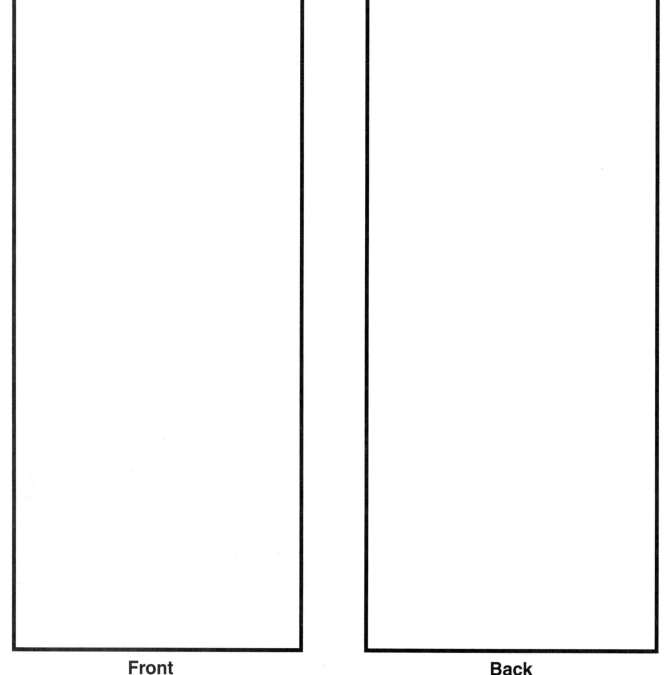

Front　　　　　　　　　　　　　　　　　**Back**

Interview

Choose a friend with whom to complete this activity.

Either you or your friend will pretend to be a television reporter. The other person will pretend to be one of the four children who has found a golden ticket. It is the reporter's job to ask appropriate questions that the television viewers will be interested in hearing answered. It is the interviewee's job to assume the role of the character chosen and answer as the character would answer. It may help the reporter to use the form below to prepare questions prior to the interview. Then, using the spaces provided, record the questions and answers during the interview.

Name of reporter: _____

Name of child: _____

Reporter: _____

_____

Answer: _____

_____

Reporter: _____

_____

Answer: _____

_____

Reporter: _____

_____

Answer: _____

_____

Reporter: _____

_____

Answer: _____

_____

Reporter: _____

_____

Answer: _____

_____

Your Family History

Charlie Bucket lives in a house along with his extended family. This means that not only does Charlie live with his mother and father, but he also lives with both sets of grandparents. Charlie considers himself very lucky to have his grandparents living with him. Often, in the evening, they tell Charlie stories that fascinate and delight him. Although Charlie loves all his grandparents, he shares a special relationship with Grandpa Joe. Together they share a wonderful adventure!

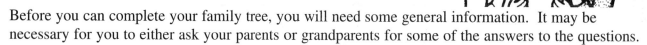

Families are important to us, and learning all about your family can be a fun activity. In this lesson, you will become a genealogist. A genealogist is a person who studies a family's history. This activity will help you learn more about your own family's history.

Before you can complete your family tree, you will need some general information. It may be necessary for you to either ask your parents or grandparents for some of the answers to the questions.

- What is your full name? Were you named after anyone?

- When were you born? Where were you born?

- What are your parents' full names? When and where were they born?

- Do you have any brothers or sisters? When and where were they born?

- What are your grandparents' full names? When and where were they born?

- Do you have other family, such as stepparents, aunts, uncles, or cousins you want to include on a family tree? If so, get the information about them.

Now, use this information to create your own family tree by filling in either the square, oval, or leaf on page 19. Look at the examples and decide which would be most appropriate for your family.

Your Family Tree

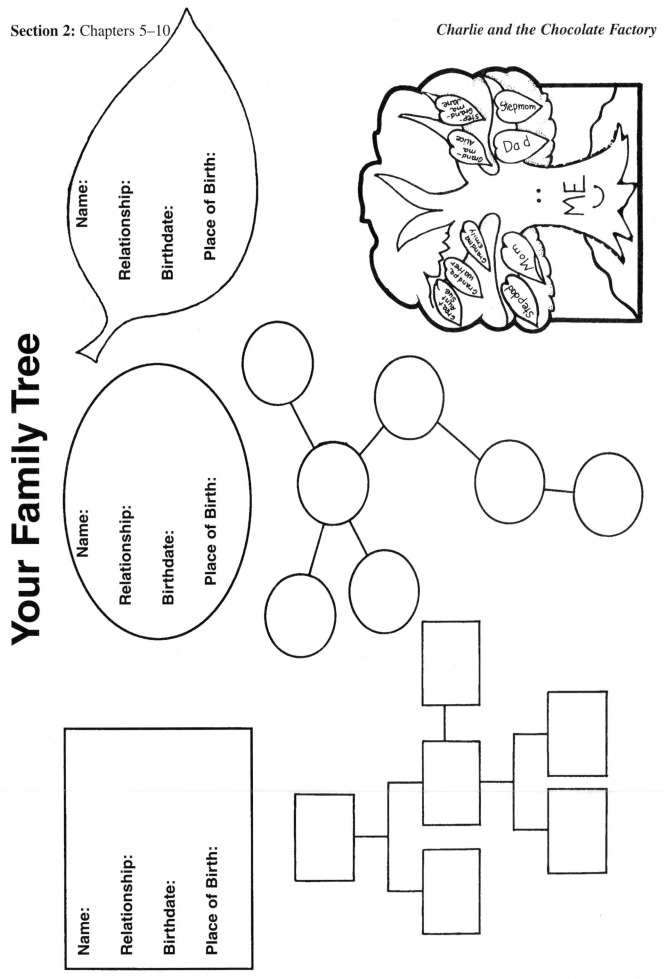

Name:

Relationship:

Birthdate:

Place of Birth:

Name:

Relationship:

Birthdate:

Place of Birth:

Name:

Relationship:

Birthdate:

Place of Birth:

Quiz Time!

1. On the back of this page, write a one-paragraph summary of the main events that happen in each of the chapters in this section.

2. What events lead to Charlie finding the golden ticket?_____

_____

_____

3. Why does the family choose Grandpa Joe to accompany Charlie to the chocolate factory?

_____

_____

4. If you were in Charlie's position, who in your family would you choose to go with you? Why?

_____

_____

5. Who works for Mr. Wonka in the factory? Do you think he can trust them? _____

_____

_____

6. How do all the children behave once they are inside the chocolate factory? _____

_____

_____

7. What do Oompa-Loompas love to eat? What is made from their favorite food? _____

_____

_____

8. What happens to Augustus Gloop? _____

_____

_____

9. Why do you think Roald Dahl chose five children to be the winners of the contest rather than five adults? _____

_____

_____

10. In light of what happened to Augustus Gloop, do you think Mr. Wonka regrets letting the children visit the factory? _____

_____

_____

Personality Profiles

Now that you have read a good portion of the book, you probably have a good idea of the character development. Each of the five children who found golden tickets have distinct personalities. Yet, in some ways they are very much alike.

Think carefully about each of the five children who visit Mr. Wonka's factory. List as many details about their personalities as you can in the boxes provided. Then answer the questions below.

Charlie	Veruca	Mike

Augustus	Violet

1. List the ways in which these five children are alike._____

_____

_____

2. List the ways in which these five children are different._____

_____

_____

3. Who is your favorite character and why? _____

_____

_____

Fantasy Story

(Part Two: Characterization)

After completing the previous assignments, you should be fairly familiar with character development. In this activity, you will develop the characters you will use when writing your fantasy story. Before beginning this lesson, review your notes from the previous assignment in which you decided on the setting of your story. You will want to choose characters appropriate to the setting.

Look at the words you used to describe the five characters in the previous assignment. You were able to give specific answers because of Roald Dahl's precise way of describing the characters in his stories. Think about Dahl's technique as you determine the characters for your story.

Decide on three characters for your fantasy story.

Decide on a particular characteristic that you will use in developing the character in your story. For example, in *Charlie and the Chocolate Factory*, Veruca Salt was a spoiled girl and Mike Teavee did nothing but watch television.

Use the excerpt below as an example to help you in describing all the characteristics of your characters. Notice how Roald Dahl's descriptions are so detailed you could draw a picture from reading his words. Remember to save this work for the next assignment.

Mr. Wonka was standing all alone just inside the open gates of the factory. And what an extraordinary little man he was! He had a black top hat on his head. He wore a tail coat made of beautiful plum-colored velvet. His trousers were bottle green. His gloves were pearly gray. And in one hand he carried a fine gold-topped walking cane. Covering his chin, there was a small neat pointed black beard—a goatee. And his eyes—his eyes were most marvelously bright. They seemed to be sparkling and twinkling at you all the time. The wholeface, in fact, was alight with fun and laughter.

Now write descriptions of the three characters you have chosen. Draw a picture of each character. Remember to keep your character descriptions for your fantasy story.

The Chocolate Room

In chapter 15, Roald Dahl describes the chocolate room in detail. Using his descriptions and some ideas of your own, complete the drawing of the chocolate room below.

Do the Right Thing

Throughout the story, Charlie has to face making some difficult decisions. In most cases, he has no one to talk with, so he relies on his own conscience for advice on what to do. Pretend that you are Charlie's best friend. Write him a note and advise him on the following issues.

1. Grandpa Joe gives Charlie a dime to get a Wonka chocolate bar. Grandpa Joe is hoping they might find the golden ticket. Grandpa Joe asks Charlie not to tell anyone in the family about their scheme. Do you think Charlie should keep this to himself or ask his parents if he should spend the money on candy?

Dear Charlie,

_____

_____

_____

_____

_____

2. Charlie is very lucky and finds a one dollar bill. Charlie knows that his family is at the point of starving, especially now that his father has lost his job at the toothpaste factory. Should Charlie give this money to his parents or spend it on candy? What if he hadn't found a golden ticket?

Dear Charlie,

_____

_____

_____

_____

_____

3. Once Charlie finds the golden ticket, he is offered large sums of money from people. A woman offers him five hundred dollars! Charlie's family is in desperate need of money. Should he keep the golden ticket or sell it so his family will have money to buy food?

Dear Charlie,

_____

_____

_____

_____

_____

Quiz Time!

1. On the back of this paper, write a one-paragraph summary of the major events in each of the chapters in this section.

2. What is the difference between Willy Wonka's gum and ordinary gum?_____

    _____

    _____

3. Describe what happens to Violet Beauregarde. _____

    _____

    _____

4. Why do you think Mr. Wonka pretends that he doesn't hear certain comments that the children make?_____

    _____

    _____

5. Mr. Wonka invented fizzy lifting drinks which lift you off the ground like a balloon after drinking. Once up in the air, how do you get down? _____

    _____

    _____

6. Why does Willy Wonka give cups of chocolate only to Charlie and Grandpa Joe?_____

    _____

    _____

7. What do the parents of the children think of Willy Wonka?_____

    _____

    _____

8. Violet disregards Willy Wonka's request that she not try the gum. With this in mind, do you think she deserves her fate? _____

    _____

    _____

9. How is Mr. Wonka going to save Violet? _____

    _____

    _____

10. Do you think Mr. Wonka is trying to get rid of the children? Why would he do it?_____

    _____

    _____

Predict the Future

Have you ever wished you could be a fortune teller? Well, here is your chance. Make your predictions about the following characters and situations. Share your predictions with the class. It might be fun to see which class member's predictions come true.

1. Augustus Gloop simply cannot resist the chocolate river. His stomach is growling and he simply has to have some chocolate. As he is "lapping" up the chocolate from the river, he accidently falls in. As if that isn't enough, he is quickly sucked into a pipe that leads directly to the fudge room. What do you think will happen to Augustus when he comes out of the pipe?

_____

_____

_____

2. Violet Beauregarde cannot resist gum. So, of course, when she finds out that Mr. Wonka has invented a brand new gum, she has to try it. Mr. Wonka warns her that it hasn't been properly tested yet. But, Violet does not care. She has to have the gum. To her surprise, the gum makes her turn purple from head to toe. It also makes her body swell up like a giant blueberry. Mr. Wonka orders Violet to the juicing room. What do you think will happen to her once she arrives?

_____

_____

_____

3. In the next section of this unit, you will read chapter 24. The title of this chapter is "Veruca in the Nut Room." What do you think might happen to Veruca in this chapter?

_____

_____

_____

4. Do you think something wild will also happen to Mike and Charlie? List your ideas below.

_____

_____

_____

Fantasy Story

(Part Three: Plot)

In previous assignments you decided on the setting of your story and described your characters in detail. In this lesson, you will decide on the plot for your story and then, finally, write the fantasy.

In a typical plotted story, a conflict or problem is presented. Through a series of complications, the problem reaches a climax. This climax is followed by a resolution.

Using the story map below, organize your plot with your writing group.

Setting

Characters:
Place:

Problem

Event 1

Event 2

Resolution

Ending:

You are now prepared to write your fantasy story. This should be relatively easy because you have already made the important decisions regarding setting, characters, and plot. Good luck!

Junk Food Junkies

Most children love to eat candy. It is all right to indulge in chocolate delicacies and other sweets as long as you do so in moderation. Too many sweets can cause trouble such as cavities in your teeth and add excess calories to your diet.

Junk food is food that contains many calories and few nutrients. Junk foods, other than candy, include potato chips, corn chips, and cookies. Many people eat junk food when they are bored or when they are watching television.

Use the chart below to keep track of the junk food you eat for four days. Record all the junk food you eat, when and where you eat it, and your feelings when you ate it. Then answer the questions that follow.

Day	Food	Time	Place	Feelings
1				
2				
3				
4				

1. What types of junk food do you eat most? _____

2. When were you most likely to eat junk food?_____

3. Where were you most often when you ate junk food? _____

4. What were you usually doing while eating junk food?_____

5. What can you do to change your junk food eating habits?_____

Chocoholic Recipes

Below are some quick and easy chocolate recipes. You may either choose a recipe to make at home on your own or work in groups in class to make a favorite recipe.

Quick and Easy Chocolate Pie

To make this simple recipe use a prepared graham cracker pie crust. Prepare instant chocolate pudding according to the package directions. Pour into the pie shell. Top with ready-made whipped cream. Serve and enjoy!

Cocoa

Try some homemade cocoa for a real treat. This will just "hit the spot" on a cold, blustery day. This recipe will serve about eight students.

In a saucepan mix $^1/_3$ cup (80 mL) of sugar, $^1/_3$ cup (80 mL) of cocoa powder, and $^1/_4$ teaspoon (1 mL) of salt. Add $1^1/_2$ cups (375 mL) of water. Stir constantly and bring to a boil. Stir and boil 2 minutes. Stir in $4^1/_2$ cups (about 1 L) of milk. Heat but do not boil. Add $^1/_4$ teaspoon (1 mL) of vanilla. Before serving use an egg beater or wire whisk to stir the chocolate and make foamy. Add a marshmallow or dollop of whipped cream.

Spidery Chocolate Treats

Who ever thought spiders could make such tasty morsels!

To make your Spidery Chocolate Treats you'll need an 8 ounce (180 g) milk chocolate bar, 2 cups (about 500 mL) crisp rice cereal, and $^1/_2$ cup (about 125 mL) shredded coconut.

Melt the chocolate in a double boiler. Or, use a microwave oven for 1–2 minutes at 50% power. Stir in the rice cereal and coconut. Drop mixture onto waxed paper, a teaspoonful at a time. Chill in refrigerator until set. Makes about 2 dozen.

No-Bake Chocolate Cookies

Make these easily prepared cookies to eat with your hot cocoa. All you need is a saucepan, 2 cups (500 mL) sugar, $^1/_2$ cup (125 mL) milk, $^1/_4$ lb. (113 g) butter, 5 tablespoons (75 mL) cocoa, $2^1/_2$ cups (625 mL) quick cooking oatmeal, and 2 teaspoons (10 mL) vanilla.

Mix milk, butter, sugar, and cocoa in a saucepan and bring to a boil. Cook for about $1^1/_2$ minutes. Remove from heat and add oatmeal and vanilla. Beat mixture until stiff. A scoop of peanut butter or nuts can be added, if desired. Drop onto wax paper by the teaspoonful. Allow cookies to cool before eating.

Quiz Time!

1. On the back of this page, write a one-paragraph summary of the main events that happen in each of the chapters in this section.

2. Why do the squirrels peck at Veruca's head? _____

   _____

   _____

3. What makes Willy Wonka's elevator different from ordinary elevators? _____

   _____

   _____

4. There are some fantastic candy inventions mentioned in the story. Which is your favorite and why?_____

   _____

   _____

5. Why is Charlie so well behaved during the tour of the factory?_____

   _____

   _____

6. Why don't Charlie's other grandparents want to go in the elevator? _____

   _____

   _____

7. None of the children fully recover from their mishaps. Do you think they wish they had never visited the factory?_____

   _____

   _____

8. How does Willy Wonka determine which of the five children would get his factory? Do you think this was predetermined? _____

   _____

   _____

9. What do you think Willy Wonka means when he says "they'll all come out in the wash."

   _____

   _____

10. How do you think Charlie and his family will adjust to living inside the chocolate factory with Mr. Wonka? _____

   _____

   _____

Crossword Puzzle

Across

2. Another factory that made ice cream that doesn't melt

5. Denomination of currency found by Charlie

7. Loves television

10. The Oompa-Loompas were imported from _____

13. Oompa-Loompas love to eat _____

14. Everlasting _____

16. Mr. Wonka is an_____ of candy

18. Charlie's favorite food

Down

1. Found the first golden ticket

2. Charlie found a golden ticket in a Wonka's Whipple Scrumptious _____ Delight

3. Mode of transportation from the factory to Charlie's house

4. New owner of chocolate factory

6. Veruca Salt is very_____

8. Prince _____ had a chocolate palace

9. Color of tickets to factory

11. Mr. Bucket works at a _____ factory

12. Took Charlie to factory

15. Loves chewing gum

17. Last name of author

Conduct a Taste Test

Do you think that all chocolate tastes the same? Conduct a taste test in the class to determine which brand of chocolate people choose most as their favorite. Note: Check for student allergies before conducting tests.

You will need: blindfold, two brands of chocolate bars, soda crackers, cups, and water.

Conducting the taste test:

- Blindfold the participant so he/she cannot see the chocolate.
- Allow the participant to taste one of the brands of chocolate.
- Give the participant a soda cracker and a few sips of water.
- Allow the participant to taste the other brand of chocolate.
- Record which was the participant's favorite.

Record the results of your taste test below by writing the participants' names and placing an "X" next to the brand they prefer. Answer the questions that follow.

Name	Brand 1	Brand 2

1. Which brand appears to be the most preferred among your class members?_____

    _____

    _____

2. Can you think of any reason that brand was the class' favorite? _____

    _____

    _____

3. Which brand was your favorite? Did you agree with the majority of the class?_____

    _____

    _____

Poetry

Following any mishap with the children, the Oompa-Loompas sing a song about them. Review the excerpt below of the song the Oompa-Loompas sing about Veruca Salt.

Veruca Salt, the little brute,

Has just gone down the garbage chute,

(And as we very rightly thought

That in a case like this we ought

To see the thing completely through,

We've polished off her parents, too.)

Down goes Veruca! Down the drain!

And here, perhaps, we should explain

That she will meet, as she descends,

A rather different set of friends.

Imagine that you are a child who won a golden ticket and then had something peculiar happen to you while at the factory. Describe your mishap.

_____

_____

_____

_____

Now write a poem for the Oompa-Loompas to sing that describes what happens to you. If necessary, review the four songs in your book for ideas.

_____

_____

_____

_____

_____

_____

Class Cookbook

In section 4 of this unit, there was an activity that allowed you to experiment with cooking some chocolate candy. Perhaps one of these recipes has now become your favorite chocolate treat. Or maybe you have a favorite recipe of your own.

In this lesson, each student will find a favorite chocolate candy recipe. In searching for recipes, try to find something different. For example, you might choose a recipe for chocolate candy from another country or a recipe that has been passed down in your family for years. After you have made your choice, write the recipe as neatly as possible on the recipe card below. These cards can then be cut out and assembled into a class cookbook for everyone to enjoy. Perhaps copies could be made and sold as a class fundraiser!

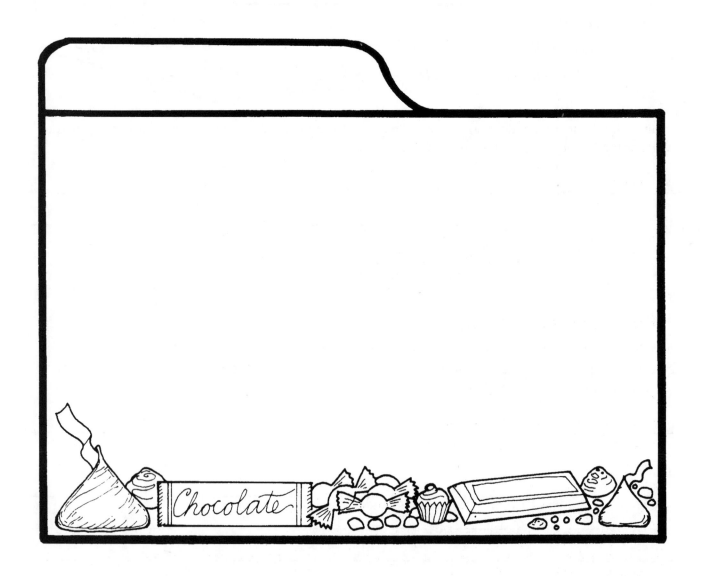

Any Questions?

When you finished reading *Charlie and the Chocolate Factory*, did you have some questions that were left unanswered? Write some of your questions here.

_____

_____

_____

Work in groups or by yourself to prepare possible answers for some, or all, of the questions you asked above and those written below. When you have finished your predictions, share your ideas with the class.

- Is Charlie able to successfully run the factory?
- What will Grandpa Joe's job be at the factory?
- Does Mr. Bucket ever go back to work at the toothpaste factory?
- Will Veruca continue to be a demanding brat?
- Will Augustus eat too much and once again become overweight?
- Does Violet give up gum chewing after her terrible ordeal?
- Will Mr. Wonka help the children recover from their mishaps?
- Is Charlie too young to learn to run a factory?
- Do you think Charlie's personality will change now that he runs the factory?
- Will the Bucket family get along with Mr. Wonka?
- What do you think was Charlie's favorite Wonka invention?
- Will Mr. Wonka's chocolate continue to be popular?
- What will become of the Oompa-Loompas?
- How will the Oompa-Loompas respond to Charlie's family?
- Will Charlie still have time to go to school?
- Will it be more important for Charlie to run the factory or go to school?
- Could Charlie get a private tutor?
- Will the family travel anywhere else in the elevator?
- What do you think would have happened if Willy Wonka had given the factory to one of the other children?
- Which other child do you think Mr. Wonka would have given the factory to?
- Do you think Charlie will ever hold a golden ticket contest when he is old?
- What if Charlie had also been bad inside the factory?
- If Mr. Wonka decided he couldn't give this factory to any of the children, do you think he would hold another golden ticket contest?
- What do you think Charlie would do if his parents decided not to move to the factory? Would Charlie still get a lifetime supply of chocolate?

Book Report Ideas

There are numerous ways to report on a book once you have read it. After you finish reading *Charlie and the Chocolate Factory*, choose one method of reporting on this book that interests you. It may be a way your teacher suggests, an idea of your own, or one of the ways mentioned below.

- **See What I Read?**

  This report is a visual one. A model of a scene from the story can be created, or a likeness of one or more of the characters from the story can be drawn or sculpted.

- **Come to Life!**

  This report is one that the lends itself to a group project. A size-appropriate group prepares a scene from the story for dramatization, acts it out, and relates the significance of the scene to the entire book. Costumes and props will add to the dramatization.

- **Into the Future**

  This report predicts what might happen if *Charlie and the Chocolate Factory* were to continue. It may take the form of a story in narrative or dramatic form or a visual display.

- **A Letter to a Character**

  In this report, you may write a letter to any character in the story. You may ask him or her any questions you wish. You may even want to offer some advice on a particular problem.

- **Guess Who or What!**

  This report is similar to "20 Questions." The reporter gives a series of clues about a character or event in the story in a vague-to-precise, general-to-specific order. After all clues are given, the character or event must be deduced.

- **Charlie Returns!**

  Write a whole new story using Charlie as the main character. Other characters from *Charlie and the Chocolate Factory* may also be used.

- **Coming Attraction!**

  Charlie and the Chocolate Factory is about to be made into a movie and you have been chosen to design the promotional poster. Include the title and author of the book, a listing of the main characters and the actors who will play them, a drawing of a scene from the book, and a paragraph synopsis of the story.

- **Literary Interview**

  This report is done in pairs. One student pretends to be a character in the story. The other student will play the role of a television or radio interviewer, providing the audience with insights into the character's personality and life. It is the responsibility of the partners to create meaningful questions and appropriate responses.

Research Ideas

Describe three things you read in *Charlie and the Chocolate Factory* that you would like to learn more about.

1. _____

2. _____

3. _____

As you are reading *Charlie and the Chocolate Factory* you will encounter culturally diverse people, distinct character types, coping techniques, and a variety of candy inventions. To increase your understanding of the characters and events in the story, as well as more fully recognize Roald Dahl's craft as a writer, research to find out more about these people and things.

Work in groups to research one or more of the areas you named above, or the areas mentioned below. Share your findings with the rest of the class in any appropriate form or oral presentation.

- Chocolate
  - history
  - how it is made
  - where it is made
  - types
  - recipes
  - nutritional value
  - cocoa beans
- Nutrition
  - junk food
  - calories
  - balanced diet
- Candy
  - types
  - recipes
  - nutritional value
- Roald Dahl
  - biographical data
  - children's books written
  - adult stories written
  - screenplays written

- Television
  - how it works
  - history
  - changes through the years
- Squirrels
  - food
  - shelling nuts
  - as pets
- Inventions
  - great inventors
  - modern inventions
- Fantasy Stories
  - popular fantasy stories
  - popular fantasy movies
- Behavior
  - manners
  - proper etiquette
- Factories
  - products
  - assembly line

Create Your Own Invention

Willy Wonka is a master at creating candy inventions. Some of the inventions he created made the following candies: chewing gum that never loses its flavor, candy balloons that blow up to enormous sizes, marshmallows that taste like violets, caramels that change colors every ten seconds, ice cream that never melts, and everlasting gobstoppers.

In this culminating activity, you will create a candy invention of your own. Use the guide below to help create your special candy, then proceed with the rest of the activity.

Brainstorm using this cluster to think of some ideas for your special candy.

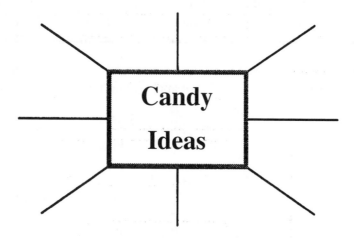

Choose an idea from above and explain why you decided to use it as your special candy-making invention.

_____

_____

Why will children like your special candy?

_____

_____

List the ingredients needed to make your special candy. Then, explain how it is made.

_____

_____

_____

Create Your Own Invention *(cont.)*

Making your candy recipe alone and by hand would be very time consuming. Let's assume there is a large demand for your candy in the stores. Store owners are calling in with orders every minute. You will need to design a machine that can make the candy for you.

Using your own drawings and the shapes below, create a machine that will make your candy. Be prepared to explain how the machine works.

Create Your Own Invention *(cont.)*

As consumers we see many ads on television each day. In an hour-long television program there can be up to 15 minutes of commercials. How do you suppose these commercials affect our buying habits? Think about it; then answer the questions below.

Have you ever wanted to buy something after seeing a commercial for the product? What was it?

_____

_____

Companies often will have an advertising agency write a "jingle" or song for their product so the consumer will remember it. Some of the jingles become quite catchy and you may find yourself humming the tune all day long.

Can you think of any jingles for products you have seen advertised recently?

_____

_____

Now that you have developed your own candy, it is necessary for you to advertise so the public will be aware of your product. Write a jingle that could be used in a television advertisement for your candy. Be as creative as possible.

Create Your Own Invention *(cont.)*

There are several decisions left for you to make regarding your new invention. Once you answer the questions below, you will be ready to begin production of your special candy!

Packaging of your product is very important. Sometimes the packaging alone will catch the consumer's eye and create interest in your product. For this reason, take time to design the wrapper for your candy. Remember, you will want to draw attention to your product.

For all your hard work in creating your special candy, you will want to be sure it is priced correctly in order for you to make a profit. It is now time for you to determine a price for your candy. You must keep in mind that if your candy is priced higher than all the others, consumers may not want to buy it. On the other hand, if it is priced too low, your profits will be less. Do a comparison of candy using the chart to the right.

Candy	Cost

Thinking about these two factors, what price will you give your candy and why?

_____

_____

Although you have already written a jingle for your product, you may also want to create a slogan. For example most of us are familiar with the slogan for M&Ms®: "Melts in your mouth, not in your hands." Create a slogan for your product and write it below.

Vocabulary Review

Use this puzzle to review the vocabulary in the story.

Across

1. Paralyzed with terror
9. One who creates something
10. Angry
13. A large boat
15. Mentally quick
17. Let down
21. Bunched together
22. Enormous in size
23. A hoodlum
24. Inspiring a sense of mystery
25. Strange or odd

Down

2. One who dances and spins wildly
3. A mass of bubbles
4. To judge the faults
5. Wishing to have someone else's things
6. An intensely hot, enclosed place
7. A loud shrill outcry
8. Living in misery
11. Decision reached by a jury
12. Characterized by rapid nervous action
14. Surprise
16. Disgusting
18. Brink of a dangerous situation
19. Extreme in degree
20. An early period of development
21. A narrow hallway

Unit Test

Matching: Match the names of the characters with their fate at the factory.

1. _____ Charlie   a. was pecked by squirrels

2. _____ Augustus Gloop   b. drank from the chocolate river

3. _____ Violet Beauregarde   c. was awarded the chocolate factory

4. _____ Veruca Salt   d. loves television

5. _____ Mike Teavee   e. was turned into a blueberry

True or False: Write true or false next to each statement.

1. _____ Charlie asked his parents if he could buy candy with the dollar he found.

2. _____ Charlie's grandparents were anxious to ride in the glass elevator.

3. _____ Mr. Wonka created the contest to find someone to take over his factory.

4. _____ Mr. Wonka encouraged the children to try new inventions at his factory.

5. _____ Mr. Salt hired workers to find tickets in thousands of chocolate bars.

6. _____ Mr. Wonka saved the Oompa-Loompas from death.

7. _____ The shopkeeper tried to get the golden ticket from Charlie.

Short Answer: Provide a short answer for each of these questions.

1. Why do Charlie's parents want Grandpa Joe to go to the factory?_____

    _____

2. Approximately how old are Charlie's grandparents? _____

    _____

3. Why doesn't Charlie sell the golden ticket to the highest bidder? _____

    _____

4. How does Charlie get the money to buy a candy bar? _____

    _____

5. How is Mr. Wonka going to get Charlie's grandparents to the factory?_____

    _____

Essay: Answer these questions on the back of this paper.

1. Describe the difference between Charlie's lifestyle and upbringing, and Veruca Salt's. How did that difference effect their fate at the factory?

2. Why do you suppose Mr. Wonka never had a family of his own?

Response

Explain the meaning of each of these quotations from *Charlie and the Chocolate Factory*.

Chapter 3   *"'All factories have workers streaming in and out of the gates in the mornings and evenings—except Wonka's! Have you ever seen a single person going into that place — or coming out?'"*

Chapter 4   *"'The faint shadows that sometimes appear behind the windows, especially late at night when the lights are on, are those of tiny people, people no taller than my knee.'"*

Chapter 6   *"'Eating is his hobby you know. That's all he's interested in. But still, that's better than being a hooligan and shooting off zip guns and things like that in his spare time, isn't it?'"*

Chapter 7   *"'He spoils her and no good can ever come from spoiling a child like that, Charlie, you mark my words.'"*

Chapter 8   *"'She'll come to a sticky end one day, chewing all that gum, you see if she doesn't.'"*

Chapter 8   *"'Just as sure as I'll be having cabbage soup for supper tomorrow, that ticket'll go to some nasty little beast who doesn't deserve it!'"*

Chapter 10   *"'He's a fine little fellow. He deserves better than this.'"*

Chapter 12   *"'I believe that the person who really deserves to go most of all is Grandpa Joe himself. He seems to know more about it than we do.'"*

Chapter 14   *"'But down here, underneath the ground, I've got all the space I want. There's no limit —so long as I hollow it out.'"*

Chapter 17   *"'My poor Augustus! They'll be selling him by the pound all over the country tomorrow morning.'"*

Chapter 18   *"'She wants a good kick in the pants.'"*

Chapter 21   *"'But I don't want a blueberry for a daughter.'"*

Chapter 23   *"'My dear old fish, go and boil your head.'"*

Chapter 24   *"'They're testing her to see if she's a bad nut.'"*

Chapter 30   *"'You see, my dear boy, I have decided to make you a present of the whole place. As soon as you are old enough to run it, the entire factory will become yours.'"*

Conversations

Work in size appropriate groups to write and perform the conversations that might have occurred in each of the following situations.

- Mr. and Mrs. Bucket decide who should go to the factory with Charlie. (2 people)

- The other grandparents discuss whether or not Joe should go with Charlie. (3 people)

- Grandpa Joe and Charlie anticipate the day of their visit to the factory. (2 people)

- Charlie's family is wondering how their day at the factory is going. (5 people)

- Mr. Wonka tells the Oompa-Loompas about the visitors. (5+ people)

- Mr. Wonka tells reporters about his plan to have visitors in the factory. (4 people)

- Oompa-Loompas discuss their feelings about visitors. (7+ people)

- Charlie's parents tell him how to behave at the factory. (3 people)

- Veruca tells her friends about finding the golden ticket. (3+ people)

- Violet and her parents discuss how she has turned blue and what they will do about it. (3 people)

- Augustus tells a reporter what it was like in the factory. (2 people)

- Mike and his parents talk to a lawyer about Mr. Wonka's recklessness. (4 people)

- Mr. and Mrs. Bucket discuss whether it is wise to move to the factory. (2 people)

- Mr. Wonka talks to Charlie about what it will be like when he takes over. (2 people)

- The family thanks Charlie for his behavior which caused them to have good fortune. (7 people)

- Charlie tells his classmates that he is moving to the factory. (7+ people)

- Mr. Wonka gives the family a tour of the factory. (8 people)

- Charlie's family decides what to eat first at the factory. (7 people)

- The Oompa-Loompas welcome Charlie's family to the factory. (8+ people)

- Charlie discusses with Grampa Joe his hopes that he will do a good job and his family can live in the factory forever. (2 people)

- A friend asks Charlie if he can live in the factory, too. (2 people)

- Charlie's parents thank Mr. Wonka for his generosity. (3 people)

Write and perform one of your own conversation ideas for the characters from *Charlie and the Chocolate Factory.*

Bibliography

Related Stories:

Babbitt, Natalie. *Kneeknock Rise.* (Farrar, Straus, and Giroux, 1970)

Babbitt, Natalie. *Tuck Everlasting.* (Farrar, Straus, and Giroux, 1975)

Banks, Lynne Reid. *The Indian in the Cupboard.* (Doubleday, 1980)

Blume, Judy. *Freckle Juice.* (Dell, 1971)

Carroll, Lewis. *Alice's Adventures in Wonderland.* (Puffin, 1946)

Du Bois, William Pene. *The Twenty-One Balloons.* (Penguin, 1986)

Grahame, Kenneth. *The Wind in the Willows.* (Scribner, 1908)

Juster, Norton. *The Phantom Tollbooth.* (Random House, 1961)

Kingsley, Charles. *The Water Babies.* (Puffin, 1984)

Lewis, C.S. *The Lion, the Witch, and the Wardrobe.* (Macmillan, 1950)

Norton, Mary. *The Borrowers.* (Harcourt, 1953)

Paterson, Katherine. *Bridge to Terabithia.* (Harper and Row, 1987)

Other Books by Roald Dahl:

Charlie and the Great Glass Elevator. (Knopf, 1972)

Danny the Champion of the World. (Knopf, 1975)

Fantastic Mr. Fox. (Knopf, 1970)

James and the Giant Peach. (Knopf, 1964)

The Witches. (Penguin, 1985)

Nonfiction:

Allarnand, Pascale. *Cocoa Beans to Daisies.* (Frederick Warne and Company, 1978)

Mitgutsch, Ali. *From Cocoa Bean to Chocolate.* (Carolrhoda Books, Inc., 1975)

Perl, Lila. *The Great Ancestor Hunt.* (Clarion Books, 1989)

Wolfman, Ira. *Do People Grow on Family Trees?* (Workman Publishing, 1991)

Answer Key

Page 10

1. Accept appropriate responses.

2. Charlie's father is the only member of the family who works.

3. Charlie lives near the chocolate factory and chocolate is his favorite food.

4. Wonka makes marshmallows that taste like violets, caramels that change colors, chewing gum that doesn't lose flavor, etc.

5. The house melted from the sun.

6. No one ever enters or leaves the factory.

7. There were spies in Wonka's factory.

8. Accept appropriate responses.

9. Charlie's family is very close. They take care of each other.

10. Accept appropriate responses.

Page 15

1. Accept appropriate responses.

2. He created the contest to find someone to take over the factory.

3. Accept appropriate responses. Some important details include: Augustus is overweight and greedy, Veruca is very spoiled by her parents, Violet chews gum all day, Mike watches television constantly, and Charlie is well behaved.

4. Accept appropriate responses.

5. Grandpa Joe wants Charlie to buy candy in hopes of finding a golden ticket.

6. Charlie's family thinks the children who have found golden tickets are spoiled brats.

7. Charlie has little energy because he doesn't get enough to eat.

8. Charlie found a dollar on the ground.

9. Accept appropriate responses.

10. Accept appropriate responses.

Page 20

1. Accept appropriate responses.

2. Charlie found a dollar and decided to buy a candy bar. Then, he decided to buy another. In the second was the golden ticket.

3. Grandpa Joe knows all about the factory.

4. Accept appropriate responses.

5. The Oompa-Loompas work for Mr. Wonka. They appear to be loyal and trustworthy.

6. All the children except for Charlie are brats and do not listen to Mr. Wonka.

7. Oompa-Loompas love to eat cocoa beans which are used to make chocolate.

8. Augustus Gloop falls in the river and is sucked through a pipe.

9. Accept appropriate responses.

10. Accept appropriate responses.

Page 25

1. Accept appropriate responses.

2. Willy Wonka's gum is a full meal.

3. Violet ate the gum and turned purple. She also blew up like a blueberry.

4. Accept appropriate responses.

5. You have to burp to get down.

6. Charlie and Grandpa Joe looked hungry.

7. The parents think Mr. Wonka is a little crazy.

8. Accept appropriate responses.

9. Mr. Wonka wants to de-juice Violet.

10. Accept appropriate responses.

Answer Key *(cont.)*

Page 30

1. Accept appropriate responses.

2. The squirrels are trying to tell if she is a bad nut.

3. Willy Wonka's elevator can travel in all directions not just up and down.

4. Accept appropriate responses.

5. Charlie has been brought up to be well mannered and well behaved.

6. Charlie's grandparents are afraid of the elevator.

7. Accept appropriate responses.

8. Because Charlie was the only child left, he will get the factory.

9. Perhaps he means it will all work out in the end.

10. Accept appropriate responses.

Page 31

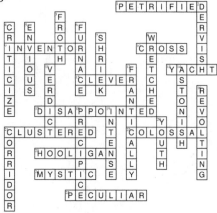

Pages 38–41

Create a class display of these inventions.

Page 42

Page 43

Matching

1) C   2) B   3) E   4) A   5) D

True or False

1. False - Charlie did not ask his parents.

2. False - Charlie's grandparents were afraid.

3. True.

4. False - Mr. Wonka told the children not to try anything that hadn't been tested.

5. True.

6. True.

7. False - The shopkeeper told Charlie to keep the golden ticket.

Short Answer

1. Grandma Joe knew all about the factory and really wanted to go.

2. Charlie's grandparents are in their nineties.

3. Charlie wanted to be able to visit the factory and have all the chocolate he could eat for the rest of his life.

4. Charlie found a dollar.

5. Mr. Wonka took the grandparents to the factory on the great elevator.

Essay

1. Accept appropriate responses. Answers should reflect how Veruca was spoiled and is used to getting everything she wants. She is also used to not listening to her parents or accepting authority. Charlie is the absolute opposite.

2. Accept appropriate responses. Answers should be creative and reflect thought by the student.

Page 44

Accept all reasonable and well-supported answers.

Page 45

Perform the conversations in class. Ask students to respond to the conversations in several different ways, such as, "Are the conversations realistic?" or "Are the words the characters say in keeping with their personalities?"